TRIPPING IN THE **DARKNESS**

TRIPPING IN THE DARKNESS
SEARCHING FOR THE LIGHT

MARGAUX B. SCOTT

ISBN: 979-8-9919813-1-6

DEDICATION

I dedicated this book to my mom, because she has stuck with me through all of life's many road bumps while never judging and always accepting me. You are my best friend and my biggest supporter of anything I have aspired to do, and you make me feel brave enough to follow my dreams, even if I do not have the confidence in myself to do so. I have no idea what I would do without you always cheering me on and reminding me of my abilities. So, thank you Mom, I love you.

TABLE OF CONTENTS

ACKNOWLEDGEMENTS

I want to thank all of you for standing by my side in life and supporting this book. Whether you've helped with ideas, or even just had words of encouragement to follow through with this, I thank you. A special shoutout to those that took the time to be my editors, but I truly appreciate all of you, and without you guys, this book would not have been made.

Jacquelyn Scott
James Quinn
Tara LaMarre
Jacqlyn Andolfo
Bridgette Norell
Kristen Nagle
Christine Dallaire
James Kalenderian
Alexandra Hutton
Nicole McIntyre
Priscilla Wille
Katie Sweet
Becky Stringham
Robert Marcelonis
Matt Smith
Vincent Andolfo
Megan Aldana

Also, I want to thank my family for any support they have given throughout the years.

TRIPPING IN THE DARKNESS

ZOMBIE

I'm not living,
I'm just dead inside,
wandering like a zombie,
with no clear path.
Yet my skin is still warm,
but my heart is too far gone,
from taking so many hits,
and destroying who I was,
until I went insane.
Now none of me remains,
and I've forgotten who I was.
So, I walk around emotionless,
and disconnected from the world,
while still trying to find a pulse,
and return to who I was.
If only I could remember,
but I'm too far gone,
stuck in this ugly form,
of this shattered person.
Unbeknownst to everyone,
that I've already died,
and the person they're seeing,
is no longer me,
just a hollow version,
of who I used to be.

THE MONSTER

There's a monster living inside my mind,
and destroying all the things that define me.
Poisoning my mind and playing tricks on me,
while gradually stealing all my happy memories.
But just when I find the exit door, it's blocked,
filled with bricks that lead nowhere.
I can't escape from the monster inside my mind,
because it hides dormant waiting years for me,
and always returns and wreaks havoc on me.
Even though I've spent years building up my defenses,
and just when I think my strategies are foolproof,
it finds my weak points and dismantles me,
while slowly breaking through my walls of sanity.
But once it has entered my mind, I'm no longer safe,
for its sharp talons have a strong hold on me,
and I'm thrown in a cage of torture with no end in sight.
Now my screams are muffled, and nobody can hear me,
and I'm unable to think or breathe,
while slowly being crushed repeatedly.
Beaten down and weak, the monster controls me.
But why does the monster always come back to torture me?
I catch my reflection, and I see that the monster is me,
and no matter what I do, the monster will always find me,
because I am the monster, and the monster is me.

SKIN AND BONES

I'm made of bones, organs, blood, and flesh,
but what makes me different from all the rest?
It's all those parts you can't physically touch,
like my heart, goofiness, and imagination.
But what if those parts slowly were destroyed,
and who I was started to fade.
Would I stay me if they disappeared completely?
Like a hairline fracture being whittled away
from continuous hits of trauma.
The fracture would never have time to heal,
while it got more deformed until it broke completely.
Because I think that person, I used to be is no longer me,
but instead of different parts defining me,
all that's left are bones, organs, blood, and flesh,
with a cavern of emptiness inside my chest,
that housed all the special parts of me,
where there once lived a real person.
Not just an impersonator who's always hurting,
no longer recognizable by even me.

WARZONE

My mind is a warzone,
and my thoughts are the bombs.
They detonate without warning,
scattering explosions all around.
All my thoughts get corrupted,
by getting scrambled from all the noise,
and each missile to my brain,
tricks me into believing I'm insane.
Then my mind goes in a loop,
repeating all my mistakes,
which causes radiation levels to rise.
Suddenly my identity is under attack,
and I'm questioning who I am.
Completely tearing myself apart,
while my nervous system shuts down,
from all the mixed signals in my brain.
So, every alarm is going off,
placing my organs on red alert,
while seizing the functionality of my body,
and speeding up the destruction of my mind.
Now no white flags can be raised,
and there's no rescue in sight,
because I'm just a ticking time bomb,
waiting for the ultimate implosion.

CONFUSION

My world is on fire,
and my mind is racing,
with thoughts moving so fast,
nothing makes any sense.
Everything happened so quickly,
it was impossible to keep up,
now nothing is familiar,
and the confusion is too much.
I'm weakened by the change,
and forgetting how to breathe,
or even how to live.
I'm screaming so loudly,
just hoping to be heard,
while falling apart,
and losing track of all my thoughts.
For my mind is full of quicksand,
and I feel completely stuck.
My fear is rising,
but with no plan to escape,
a new me is forming.
An unlikeable version,
because the old me is dying,
and it's too late to be saved.
My body is cold,
and my heart is missing.
But my mind is trapped,
inside a dead body,
no longer in control,
just watching my life unfold.

THE PERFORMER

Rest in peace to my happiness,
I think I reached the point of no return.
My broken pieces are too shattered,
from slowly cracking over time.
Now there is no trace of my former self,
drifting around like an empty shell.
Darkness hidden behind a perfect smile,
makeup concealing the pain behind my eyes.
I've been putting on a 5-star performance,
the most perfect the world has ever seen.
But my walls are finally collapsing,
and all my darkness is seeping out.
Soon the makeup will come off,
and they will finally see me,
but will they still like me?
Will they still come out to the show?
Because I've been masquerading as a comedy,
soon to be seen as a tragedy,
just a living body with a dead soul,
completely lost in the darkness.
No longer able to give a phony performance,
because all my personality is gone,
and all that's left are memories of who I used to be.

BROKE ME

Everyone took a turn,
as they tore out my heart,
piece by piece,
until they broke me.
They took away my essence,
while I tried to be strong,
and not forget who I was.
Until I completely fell apart,
from being belittled too much.
Now all my trust is gone,
and there are walls around my heart,
so that way nobody can hurt me.
But the damage has been done,
and the best parts of me are gone,
they withered away,
while I tried to stay strong.
Now I'm completely lost,
and I feel like I am nothing,
just like a ghost, no longer living.
Because there was no mercy,
just a series of blows,
that directly hit my heart.
My character was attacked,
and all the facts got twisted,
which made me question myself.
Now I'm what everyone made me,
a broken-hearted version,
of who I once was.

BULLET TO THE BRAIN

Nonsensical thoughts start creeping in,
like a bullet to the brain,
as an uneasy feeling takes over.
My body is tingly,
and my chest is tight.
Images in my mind become unclear,
and my thoughts are out of control.
Suddenly, I feel psychotic,
like I belong in a padded room,
as a patient of an asylum.
Because my body is numb,
and my vision is failing.
Everything is blurry,
and my chest feels tighter.
I'm running out of air,
and I feel frozen.
Completely trapped,
and unable to process
any mental requests.
Because nothing feels real,
and the connections in my brain,
have all been severed.
So, I'm lost in my own mind,
with no lifeline in sight,
imprisoned in a world of insanity.

MURDERED

There's blood on my hands,
and I think I've been murdered.
For a twisted version of me has taken over.
Because I was knocked to the ground,
and beaten down for too long,
until eventually I turned on myself,
because I thought I was a demon.
So, I attacked myself,
because I only saw my negative ways,
until I was no longer recognizable,
becoming everything I never wanted to be.
Then I eventually became everything I hated,
because that's how they viewed me,
and I took all their words as fact.
Now I really miss myself,
and I'm grieving everything I was,
and all the things I thought I could be.
So, I'm only filled with darkness,
for all the lights have been turned off,
because I was stabbed in the heart.
However, the lethal blow was done by me,
because I was tricked into killing myself,
and destroying everything good about me.
It was an accidental suicide,
for I was guided to my grave,
and fooled into thinking I was a demon.
Made to believe I was nothing,
and everything was beaten out of me,
now there's nothing left.
So, say hello to the new me,
I don't think they're going to like me,
but hey that's what they made me.

IDENTITY CRISIS

Going through an identity crisis,
for I think I've shattered my core,
and who I was is no longer,
but who am I now?
This person is so unfamiliar,
with traits I don't know.
So, I keep looking inside,
for that old familiar feeling,
but it's all been abandoned,
nothing but empty space now.
Because there's nothing to recognize,
just echoes of my former self.
And all that's left is discomfort,
it's like my skin is crawling,
just itching to remember,
that person I used to be.
However, the memory has faded,
it's completely lost in the past.
For that person I used to cherish,
is now impossible to find.
So, it's time for a memorial,
for the death of who I used to be.
Might as well bury me,
because I'm no longer me.

The Mirror

I spent too much time looking in the mirror,
now my reflection is getting blurry.
The more I focus, the deeper the cracks appear,
but it's getting harder to see myself clearly.
Then one final squint and it's all in pieces,
shattered and broken on the floor.
The pieces that used to define me,
have razor sharp edges that slice to the touch.
Now just a distorted puzzle without instructions,
with pieces too broken to fit back together.
So, a fractured reflection appears on the floor,
resembling someone that looked like me.
However, the eyes are all wrong,
they're pitch black and hollow,
for light is no longer visible in them.
The smile is completely missing,
and the rest of the face is fuzzy,
while nothing else is recognizable.
All that's left is a fragmented impression,
of my former reflection.

PLASTIC DOLL

I feel like a plastic doll,
with a painted-on smile.
Not capable of frowning,
because I wasn't designed that way.
But what if the plastic cracked,
and a frown shined through.
Would my value go down,
for being less fun to play with?
Becoming another toy discarded,
and no longer what everyone wanted.
Nobody wants to think about the darkness,
the well-kept secrets hidden under the smile.
So, I give the world a picture-perfect image,
the doll that everyone wants.
Because nobody likes defective dolls,
the ones that can't be fixed.
They're more trouble than they're worth,
always getting placed on the back of the shelf,
right before the clearance bin,
just waiting to be forgotten.

DISAPPEARING

My thoughts are so heavy,
the weight is too much,
feels like I'm sinking,
drowning under my thoughts.
Everything is scrambled,
and my happiness is fading,
but was it ever here?
There's never any relief,
for all the comfort is gone,
even in a crowded room,
I feel so alone.
For I'm disappearing,
and soon I'll be invisible,
because I've lost my spirit,
and I'm only living for others,
not caring to live for myself.
I think I've disappeared,
but only under the surface,
it's just nobody can see,
what's really been going on.
I didn't want to be a burden,
or knew who to trust,
so I held everything in,
until my thoughts ripped me apart.
Now I'm completely broken,
and I've disappeared from myself.

THE GIRL

Who is the girl that I used to be?
I feel like she was taken from me.
She carried the world on her back,
but her bones began to snap.
Though she tried to keep it together,
while her world fell apart,
the weight was too much to hold.
Broken from the outside world,
she became a shattered mess,
and her inner spirit withered away.
What remained was a frail body with a weak soul,
an empty vessel filled only with pain.
Her once strong heart is missing,
now scars and bruises have taken their place,
and her eyes are sunken and black as the sea.
Oh, where is the girl that I used to be,
is she nothing but a distant memory?

MIND DYSPHORIA

Body dysmorphia of the mind,
I can't seem to recognize myself.
This life I lead feels so foreign,
everything is different, nobody is the same.
I'm trapped in a different dimension,
but when did I leave mine?
I'm not the same,
identical voice, and similar eyes,
but so different on the inside.
What happened to me, where did I go?
Everything feels out of place,
and my life feels out of focus.
There's no clear picture in my mind,
memories of the past aren't even mine.
So, I'm uncomfortable in my skin,
longing for a connection,
to a life filled with comfort,
and a recognizable face in the mirror.
Even in times of chaos one thing remained,
familiarity in the pain, but that's gone too.
For I'm completely fading away,
and losing the connections to my life,
while feeling utterly alone,
because something died in me.
Now I'm being reborn into something new,
but this isn't growth, it's a lesser form,
of someone I don't like, in a life I don't know.
Completely detached from reality,
just grieving the old me,
and a life that felt like mine.

MADNESS IN MY BRAIN

My flame's slowly burning out,
I'm circling the drain.
I wish there was someone to blame,
for all this madness in my brain.
Because I long to feel something,
a little heartbeat in my chest,
and not feel so alone,
or at least more like myself.
Because this isn't me,
I've been pushing everyone away,
without a second thought.
Surrounding myself with walls,
because I'm scared of all the pain,
that others can bring.
But the disconnection is too much,
and I'm drifting away,
from everyone I love.
Because I no longer trust others,
or even myself,
for all I see is the damage,
completely left in my wake.
Clouding all my judgment,
making me run away,
and driving me insane.

DETACHMENT

Displaced from my own life,
I'm shifting out of view.
Can't seem to get focus,
on who I used to be,
or what my life once was.
Whenever I try to remember,
what used to feel so familiar,
I get shivers down my spine,
overwhelmed with no connection,
when I used to live comfortably,
and my life felt like my own.
Before the detachment occurred,
from everyone, and myself.
Now I'm hard to recognize,
because my actions are so different,
and that little voice in my head,
no longer sounds the same.
It's been a slow process,
of forgetting who I am,
from getting broken over time.
For the connections in my brain,
are now entirely rewired,
making me lose touch with reality.
So, I'm barely even here,
with nothing but static in my mind,
and some broken memories.
Not sure what's real,
because it feels like a nightmare,
a living fever dream.
Everything feels wrong and out of place,
for I've drifted from everything familiar,
completely past the point of no return,
with no ability on how to adjust,
totally detached from existence.

PRISONER OF MY MIND

It's hard to care how people see me,
when I feel like a monster to myself.
The words thrown my way,
could never do the damage I could do.
I'm always berating myself,
with all these thoughts inside my head,
full of accusations and criticisms.
Yeah, I really torture myself,
but it's just so easy to do,
when I'm locked inside my mind,
because my mind is a penitentiary.
I'm always the prisoner, and the warden,
punishing myself for all my mistakes.
However, the warden's mind is made up,
I'm never giving myself a pardon.
For I'm a three-strike offender,
and there's no escaping this prison,
it's Alcatraz of the mind,
and I'm the only prisoner.

NOTHING LEFT

I think I lost a part of me,
the happy and hopeful me.
I gave away so much,
until there was nothing left.
But I always thought I'd survive,
carrying everyone's pain.
So, I gave them my light,
then I got lost in the darkness,
but nobody was there to save me.
So, what happens when the rescuer,
needs to be rescued.
Because I needed a lifeline,
and didn't know how to do it alone,
nor how to ask for any help.
For it seemed so easy at first,
to take away everyone's pain,
and carry it all on my back,
instead of swallowing them up.
However, I underestimated,
how much I could take,
until I was too far gone,
completely lost in the darkness.
For my light finally flickered out,
when I took on a little too much,
and now there's nothing left,
of what I valued so much.

DARK CLOUD

There's a dark cloud floating above my head,
growing bigger by the day.
Containing raindrops filled with sadness,
drenching all that get too close.
Slowly infecting the world around me,
making everyone just like me.
I'm a disease, a walking plague,
turning smiles into frowns.
Making everyone miserable,
while destroying happiness,
with my contagious moods.
For my disastrous nature,
forms a chain reaction of misery,
and the byproduct of my storm,
fills the sky with infinite clouds.
Blocking out the sun,
and bringing shadows all around.
Suddenly the world is filled with darkness,
and dark is the new norm.
For light feels out of place,
and happy people don't belong,
with all endlessly stuck in my storm.

THE ONCE TALL GIRL

Once there was a girl that stood so tall,
she felt she could do anything,
even take on the world.
She had a big smile,
once so full of life,
until she was made small,
by everyone around her.
Then her shoulders started to slouch,
and she no longer stood as tall,
her confidence was broken,
and the view of herself had altered.
She no longer knew who she was,
and only believed what everyone told her.
For they whispered in her ear,
all the right things to say,
to make her not okay.
Until she lost faith in her abilities,
believing she wasn't enough,
because that's what everyone told her.
They pointed out her mistakes,
and all the ways they were better,
just to keep her beneath them,
while breaking her in the process.
For they didn't want her to shine,
because then they would feel behind.
So, they destroyed her spirit,
until she was no more,
and in the end, who she was at her core.

PRETENDING

It's easier to say I'm fine,
then unload everything on my mind.
So, I throw on a smile,
and go on pretending I'm fine,
even when I'm crying inside.
So, I try to make others laugh,
and hope they'll never know,
behind the jokes is just another lost soul.
Because it's easier to say I'm great,
then burden others with the weight,
of my bad decisions,
and annoy others with my mistakes.
Because I don't want to be a problem,
nor get any extra attention,
for the pile of my misdeeds.
So, I just go on pretending,
and hope they'll never know,
how much I'm really hurting,
from all the painful things said,
that just linger in my head.
However, that pain doesn't come close,
to feeling like a burden.
So, I just go on pretending,
and hope they'll never know,
how much I'm really pretending.

PIECES LEFT BEHIND

Some of the building blocks of me are missing,
I think some of them have died.
Once again, I got lost,
drifting in the dark corners of my mind.
This place is so familiar,
I've been here dozens of times.
But every time I've come to this place,
and finally made it through to the other side,
some pieces unfortunately got left behind.
There have been so many versions of me,
each one stronger every time,
but inside the emptiness has grown,
where the whole parts of me used to reside.
All those missing pieces that got left behind,
have long been forgotten.
So, who is this new version of me?
Because I feel so unfamiliar,
and I really miss who I once was,
all the previous versions of me,
who at least felt a little more like me.
Because I think I'm being hollowed out,
piece by piece over time.
Soon there will be nothing left,
and who I was will be forgotten.
But I wonder if anyone will notice,
when I'm standing before them,
and it's no longer me.

NEW ME

Who am I,
where did I go?
I feel like I was here,
just a second ago.
Has it been long,
since I lost me?
I'm confused,
who is this?
This isn't me.
I feel so different,
then I used to be.
What happened to me,
why'd I change?
I wish I could remember,
who I used to be.
This seems unfair,
why'd I disappear?
I miss me.
I'm so uncomfortable,
with this new me.

OLD WOUNDS

Words can be like daggers,
they can slice and tear us apart,
hit deep inside and change our thoughts.
They can split us in half, ruin our identity,
and tear apart our core,
while making us forget who we are.
They're more deadly than a physical strike,
for mental abuse always hits harder,
because bones can heal,
and a cut eventually stops bleeding.
Although we may be left with scars,
the wounds within us,
are always deeper and bigger,
and they take longer to heal.
But sometimes they never do,
and a few choice words,
can rip open those old wounds,
even wider than before.
However, those old scars are harder to see,
underneath the surface,
from years of pain and defeat,
and they can easily become new wounds.
Because it's easy to believe,
if what you dislike about yourself,
is all you ever hear.
Then it's hard not to believe,
that every word is true,
if others are saying it not just you.

SURVIVAL MODE

Been in survival mode trying to see the light,
but all I see is everything dark and twisted.
Altered illusions in my mind,
unable to determine what's real,
where beauty is grotesque,
and comfort is seen as a threat.
Just a welcome invitation to be attacked,
by the ones with fake smiles.
So, the shield never gets lowered,
for if it does then it opens the door,
to get torn apart where there are no defenses.
Deep inside is where my inner child resides,
for the very last bits of me are my innocence,
and I must stay on guard to protect it.
So, a helping hand is seen as an enemy,
and good is seen as bad,
because danger is everywhere,
when you exist in survival mode.
Fight or flight instincts are always activated,
and I'm too afraid to go back into the light,
for fear it's a ruse to destroy me.
So, it's better to dance around the danger,
and I've been doing this for so long,
I've really got this rhythm down,
and my eyes have adjusted to the dark.
I think might I'm stuck like this,
but I was never going to be bright and shiny anyway.

DISTRESS

My mind is always a mix of emotions,
bringing with them physical distress,
with this tight feeling in my chest,
that feels like it's always been there.
I try to change my thought patterns,
but the feeling always stays.
Never truly feeling any peace,
while waiting for it to peak,
at the most random times,
and give me another meltdown.
Then there's no option but to dissociate,
into complete mental distress,
with bursts of irrational thoughts,
while I'm pretending to be fine,
when I'm breaking inside,
and forgetting how to trust.
So, I push everyone away,
while hiding in my corner,
of this imaginary world,
my mind created in defense.
Triggered by all the hurt inflicted,
while still craving comfort,
but not knowing how to find it,
because I'm forgetting how to attach.
So, I'm feeling all alone,
filled with confusion and internal conflict,
pushing and pulling in all directions.
Running towards comfort,
but never trusting it's real,
just waiting for another dagger,
to be wedged in my back.
So, while avoiding the possibility of pain,
I self-sabotage the possibility of love.

CONFUSION SORROW

Complicated life filled with sorrow and pain.
Open wounds left by heart's desire.
Nothing puts the pieces back together.
Failure again conquers the mind.
Unable to move on.
Scars are open and visible.
Incompleteness from my broken pieces.
On the edge of insanity.
Never going to find the answers I seek.

Sadness overcomes me.
On the brink of giving up.
Ready to lose control.
Running from myself.
Opening to the darkness.
Welcomed by death's door.

WALK AWAY

Why is it so easy for people to leave?
Get up and walk away,
like they don't even know me,
and completely desert me.
It makes me question my worth,
when I feel disposable,
but I've met me, and I get it.
I'm kind of a hassle,
a little too much to deal with,
so they can only handle so much.
Or maybe there's someone better,
that has all the qualities that I don't.
I've never been able to quite figure it out,
what exactly is wrong with me,
that people don't like.
Nor what rubs them the wrong way,
to make them run away.
Maybe it's my annoying laugh,
or how I'm too hyper, and I can't shut up.
But what I do know is that it's easy,
for them to up and walk away,
and act like I don't matter,
then replace me with another.
It's happened so many times,
going as far back as I can remember.
So, I guess that's why I think I'm annoying,
and a problem to be around.
For I'm so afraid to scare people away,
but I'm prepared for it to happen anyway.
Because I've gotten accustomed,
for people to up and walk away,
and even though it hurts every time,
I know eventually it'll happen anyway.

BEEN A LONG TIME

It feels like it's been a long time,
since I've recognized myself,
as someone I could love,
or even respect.
My thoughts feel so different,
they no longer feel like my own,
because now there's anger,
brewing deep inside of me.
I used to be able to contain it,
but now it's all spilling out.
Once it was so easy to convert it,
to an emotion I could control,
but now I don't know how,
and I'm scared of myself.
Because I don't reach out,
and bond with the ones I love.
All my trust got broken,
now there's nothing left,
but a wall wrapped around my heart.
No longer letting others in,
to who I really am.
Because my vision of me is distorted,
and it's been a long time,
since I saw myself as nice.
But really it happened overnight,
so now my self-image is corrupted,
and I'm crawling in my skin.
Because I know I'm not the same,
and I don't think I'll ever be again.

MOTIONS

Going through the motions,
but my heartbeat is slowing down.
So, I wonder if I'm still living,
or if this loop will ever end.
I've taken a backseat to my life,
while confusion has entered my mind,
and I can't seem to function,
because I think I'm dead inside.
No plans, or directions, I'm aimless,
just sifting through the rubble of my life,
trying to pick up the broken pieces,
of my old self.
For I went deep inside my mind,
looking for peace,
but lost my understanding of where I belong.
Now everything feels like it's repeating,
because every day is the same,
and I can't shake this feeling,
I'm living a déjà vu.
I'm disconnected, completely detached,
my essence feels shattered,
and I'm forgetting how to exist.
So, I just keep going through the motions,
because that's all I know how to do.

TRUSTING HAPPINESS

Trust is wearing thin,
now afraid of what happiness can bring,
the downfall and the crash.
Wanting to embrace that feeling,
but it's impossible to trust,
because as quickly as it comes,
it can easily be taken away.
So, it's better to run away,
wall up, and believe,
that this is the right way.
Pushing all the love away,
making it harder to feel that way.
Because it's best to avoid the feeling,
by not letting yourself embrace it,
then it's impossible to lose it.
So, you embrace the sadness,
removing all expectations,
that things will ever be okay.
Then you start settling in the pain,
numbness isn't far away,
and you'll trick your mind,
that it's always been this way.
But it's better than happiness,
getting completely ripped away.
But, if for a moment you feel that feeling,
best to view it as a passing phase,
and remember it's only temporary.
Then you'll be fully prepared,
when it's eventually stripped away.

LOVING ME

I'm my biggest enemy,
with the devil on my shoulder,
always telling me I've failed.
He makes it hard for me to believe,
in the possibility of love,
but not love with others,
only about loving me.
There's never an easy way to embrace it,
while he talks so negatively,
it's just impossible to feel,
because the hate slowly grows,
deep inside where the love should be.
He makes me believe I'm not good enough,
and even when I'm proud,
and it's one step forward,
he reminds me why not to be,
and it's five steps back.
So, I'm never proud,
of a single accomplishment,
because there's never a good enough reason,
to put a smile on my face,
and be proud of the work I've done.
I just don't know how to love me,
and even though I never stop trying,
there's always a reason that makes me believe,
I'm not worthy of the greatest love,
the act of truly loving me.

PAST AND PRESENT

Stay present, stay present,
isn't that what they always say?
But what if the present is so unfamiliar,
that the thought of it just makes you quiver,
as it sends you uncomfortable chills,
down every inch of your body.
So, you retreat into your mind,
back to a time that felt good, and familiar.
Staying present is easier said than done,
when it becomes so unnerving,
that it's hard to breathe.
When you feel so disconnected,
between your body and thoughts,
from all the missing parts,
that got lost along the way.
So, you hang on to memories,
repeatedly playing in your mind,
clinging on to some form of semblance,
when you were comfortable and happy.
Now only living in fear those times are gone,
how do you stay present,
when the past felt like home,
and you felt like you.

THE WAY I THINK

I don't know what's wrong with me,
and why I think like I do.
I wish there was a simple answer,
because I haven't got a clue.
But I always drive myself nuts,
thinking like I do.
For I make up wild scenarios,
that are too crazy to be true,
but I make myself believe them,
because it's just so easy to do.
But when thoughts pop in my head,
the ones I really want to be true,
then I stop believing,
they could ever be true.
The bad thoughts seem so likely,
and the good seem out of reach,
because I never let myself win,
even in my own mind.
For that would be too easy,
to have a simple mind like that,
so instead, I'm forever stuck,
thinking like I do.

LIVING IN LIMBO

I live on the edge of my seat,
waiting for the next bad thing to happen.
Never trusting things are okay,
because things keep on happening.
My world gets turned upside down,
within a moment's notice,
so, it's impossible to relax,
when I'm under all this stress.
My mind starts racing,
going over all the facts,
and the possibilities,
of all the bad things,
that could ever happen.
However, it's not paranoia,
or bouts of worry,
because when things seem okay,
that feeling of relief gets taken away.
So, I don't know how to trust the good,
when the bad is never far away.
Therefore, I live in limbo,
between the good and the bad,
the possibility of happiness,
and the probability of sadness.
So, when things go wrong,
I'm fully prepared,
and things never seem as bad.

SEARCHING FOR THE LIGHT

IF ONLY

If only I could see the way they see me,
look in the mirror and be proud of me,
and not tear myself apart with my failures,
while always getting lost in all my mistakes.
Maybe then I could be happy,
walk around with my head held high,
filled with confidence,
able to acknowledge my accomplishments.
Then maybe I would feel good enough,
and believe I'm worthy of love,
be someone that mattered and thought of,
and considered an important person.
Not always feeling like a loser,
consumed with the notion I am nothing.
Maybe then I would wake up smiling,
excited to start the day,
believing all the compliments are real,
and able to see how beautiful I really am.
Not constantly viewing myself as less than,
always thinking I'm just a problem.
But I can't see the way they see me,
even though I have spent my whole life trying.
Because all I see is everything I'm not,
and all the things I wish I could be.
If only I could see the way they see me,
I think I would really like that version of me.

ATTRACTED TO BROKEN PEOPLE

I think I'm attracted to broken people,
because their insides match mine.
Therefore, I make it my mission to heal them,
always forgetting myself in the process.
It's just so hard to look after myself,
when I see so many others in pain.
So, I put them first,
and carry their baggage on my back.
Because I think the satisfaction of healing them,
will somehow make me okay,
but I always get lost along the way.
I'm constantly identifying as a healer,
but what happens when I need healing?
Well then, I push everyone away,
because I don't want to be a burden,
by having others carry my weight.
Why is it so easy for me to help the hopeless?
But my wants and needs are never enough,
to ever put myself first.
It's because I see everyone as more important,
than I could ever be.
Thus, they are the ones that need saving,
it should never be me.
So, I stay seeking the broken,
because what am I without them,
when they help define me.

DARK PLACE

Deep inside my mind a dark place exists,
within it lives the master of deception,
offering comfort and familiarity.
It's so appealing it's hard not to embrace,
my old friend that I know so well.
Thus, any invitation back to that sinister place,
is an easy one to accept.
However, once I make my way there,
inside the labyrinths of my mind,
all the paths leading back to the light,
slowly start fading away.
I then unwillingly make my descent,
farther down the rabbit hole,
where light no longer exists.
Until I'm trapped only living in fear,
afraid of my own thoughts,
convincing me I'm monster.
They try deceiving me to stay down there,
while manipulating me with an easy way out,
by making death seem so enticing.
But I don't want to die,
I just want to live without the pain,
but the voices say I belong there.
So, I end up battling myself,
with reminders of my strength,
and the power of my lies.
Until I climb back up,
returning to the light and say farewell,
once again to that dark place.

BLOCK OUT THE WORLD

The anger builds like a wall inside my mind,
creating a powerful defense,
but the harder you push, the farther I go.
Then I'm off on my way,
on a personal journey of self-discovery.
For you never saw this outcome coming,
only thinking there'd be a little bit of space.
But I've been teetering on the edge of my own sanity,
and you just gave me a reason to leave.
Now I've walked out the door, not wanting to look back.
For I think you gave me a reason to find myself,
without the baggage of everyone else.
Because I'm always carrying others' weight,
never taking care of myself.
But it's time to finally block out the world,
and run away from the drama, and the pain.
For I'm sick of being stabbed in the back,
while trying to make sense of a senseless world.
Longing for acceptance that will never come,
nor the forgiveness that I truly deserve,
while constantly waiting for everything to feel right.
So, I'm done, and no longer will I be a people pleaser,
just waiting to be walked on,
for it's time to take care of myself.
Because I've tried to be the nice guy,
and I've tried to see it from everyone's perspective,
but it's time for me to disappear.
For the only way to find the best version of me,
is to block out the world.
Because everyone pushed me away,
and I was the problem in everyone's story.
Well now, I'll be the ghost in their story,
because I've been pushed too far,
and my limit has been reached.
It's time to finally find me.

INTRUSIVE THOUGHTS

Staring at the ceiling, hearing the clock tick away,
as the blades of the fan go round and round.
Late at night they start creeping in,
when the world goes silent and everyone's asleep,
that's when I hear them.
Running through my mind like a freight train,
intrusive thoughts are at it again.
So, I stare at the ceiling,
as time keeps on ticking.
Trying my best to drown them out,
with some nice peaceful thoughts.
Reminding myself to stop thinking,
that I'm just battling myself.
But they're so relentless,
and they keep multiplying out of control.
They're confusing me and overloading my mind,
by replaying every conversation,
and making me question every decision,
back and forth in a loop.
So, I watch the shadows on the walls,
of the cars driving by,
listening to the laughter on the television,
as I try to think about tomorrow.
But that only overwhelms me more,
because my mind is caught on a runaway train,
speeding by so fast.
These intrusive thoughts are just too much,
that even the sound on the television isn't enough,
to help drown out all the noise.
For all I can hear are my own thoughts,
until the sun comes up.
Making it just another night,
with me and my intrusive thoughts.

FIGHTING FOR MY LIFE

I'm fighting for my life,
and I've fallen so low.
I'm just so tired,
of the back and forth,
and all the mind games,
that I play with myself.
It's always such a battle,
telling myself I'm strong,
when all I feel is defeat.
I'm starting to lose hope,
and I'm fading away,
while my strength is slowly dying.
I think the weaker part of me,
is starting to take control,
and reaching for the white flag,
because I know I'm losing,
and surrendering seems easy.
Because some days are so hard,
that I want to give up.
For I could easily throw in the towel,
just give up and call it a day.
However, I'm not ready to walk away,
because I know what I'll be losing.
All the possibilities that are yet to come.
There's a future where I'm smiling,
no longer drowning in all this pain.
So, I must regain my strength,
but I know it won't be easy,
because life never is.
But I am not alone,
even if it feels that way,
I'm needed, I must not forget,
nor how much I'm loved.
I just need to have patience,
for a small sparkle of light,
that will eventually come.

TRICKSTER THOUGHTS

Thoughts can be tricksters,
making us believe what's not true,
by twisting the facts,
with made-up stories that we believe.
Because it's easy to believe lies,
especially when they come from you.
They can make you turn on yourself,
even the ones around you,
by making you think everyone is out to get you.
For it's so easy to descend into madness,
due to the irrationality of the mind,
and the thoughts that go along with it.
The mental abuse we cause ourselves,
by telling ourselves we are nothing,
with continuous thoughts of negativity,
that play on repeat.
It only fuels the narrative,
which makes it hard to separate,
the facts from the fiction.
But remembering that the mind plays games,
can help you uncover the truth,
and fighting the negativity by not letting it cycle,
stops the deceiving thoughts dead in their tracks.
For the mind can be your enemy,
but in the end, it's still your mind.
Thoughts can be pushed away,
by looking out for the traps you create for yourself,
and by remembering who you are.
Because thoughts are only as powerful,
as you allow them to be.

LOSING MY MIND

My mind is racing,
I'm pacing,
I can't sit down.
Struggling to breathe,
slowly dying,
feels like I'm six feet underground.
I think I'm losing my mind,
because everything is fading to black,
and I'm just destabilizing.
What's happening to me?
I'm no longer in touch with reality,
spinning more out of control,
completely frozen in place,
and unable to speak.
All my senses are overloading,
and I'm filling with fear,
while trying to rationalize,
all the thoughts inside my mind.
Because none of them make any sense,
deep down I know this,
but my mind got the better of me,
it happens all the time.
So, I must pull myself together,
if I want to get through this.
I'm my biggest adversary,
but the master of my own mind.

FALSE PERCEPTIONS

If only everyone didn't affect me,
then the version of me that I see,
wouldn't be their perception of me.
Too many times I let their words,
penetrate my mind,
and distort how I see me.
However, I'm better than their view of me.
But all these insecurities,
from false perceptions,
bestowed upon me,
have begun to destabilize me.
Because my defenses are weak,
from all the fractures in my walls.
Created by condescending words,
and hateful remarks,
that have hit a little too close,
to the center of my heart.
However, their words are just lies,
inside I know this.
I just need better defenses,
because I'm kind of amazing,
and the view of me,
from my perception,
is far more important,
then their opinions of me.
For I will never love me,
until I let go of all these distorted views,
that have been placed upon me.
For I know the truth,
and I should be proud just to be me.

FIRE

My mind is on fire,
there's no water in sight.
Thoughts are melting together,
and oxygen is depleting,
from my lungs burning up.
It's getting harder to breathe,
and even harder to scream.
My voice is but a whisper,
and I'm dying inside.
I feel like I'm being tortured,
this pain is unbearable.
How do I make it stop,
when every organ is on fire?
They say everything is temporary,
but I've been burning for so long.
It always stems from my brain,
then spreads like wildfire,
until I'm fully engulfed,
and riddled in pain.
However, I've been here before,
with three degree burns all over,
and completely unrecognizable.
See, the fire eventually goes out,
for I just needed time to heal,
and bandages for my wounds.
Although I'm left with a few burns,
deep inside where nobody can see,
and I may look different to me.
I always survive,
because I'm much stronger,
than I make myself out to be.

VOICES IN MY HEAD

If you could hear the voices in my head,
and all the things they say,
the way I put myself down,
when nobody is around.
I'm my toughest critic,
I'm truly harder on myself.
Because nobody knows me better,
than I know myself.
So, it's no surprise the amount of pressure,
I put on myself.
For I'm the only one,
that knows what I can achieve.
That's why I'm so hard on myself.
Because nothing is ever good enough,
and my own mind,
is always holding me back,
because of this battle in my brain.
I tell myself I can't do it,
but deep down that is a lie.
For I wish I was nicer to myself,
if only I could be more kind.
Because my mind is kind of great,
if only I could give myself a break.
For all the times I've failed,
because they're only mistakes.
So, I must keep reminding myself,
there's always room to grow,
and nobody is perfect,
stop being so hard on yourself.

SHORES OF SANITY

These waves start creeping in,
intensity set to the max.
Taking over my body,
causing my mind to fill with doubt.
Can't figure out why,
but I get overtaken so quickly,
and there's no way to stop it,
completely losing control.
Now my body feels alien,
except for this painful sensation,
I feel all over me.
As my breathing gets shallow,
while trying to think clearly,
but feeling no peace.
For my thoughts are insane,
and corrupting all the pathways,
to normal thinking behavior.
So, I'm lost in the chaos,
that used to be my mind,
while trying to find a thought,
that makes any sense,
to help me navigate back,
where I am in control.
No longer feeling knives in my chest,
with regulation back to my breathing.
Once I grasp a peaceful thought,
the pain slowly recedes,
and my thoughts get a bit clearer.
The waves get smaller,
and I return to the shores of sanity,
where my mind makes sense,
and my body feels like my own.

THE DOOR

There's a door inside my mind filled with darkness,
and sometimes I get tempted and open it,
accidentally letting out all my demons.
They try relentlessly to consume my thoughts,
by attacking my mind on repeat,
while making me forget that I'm in control.
For I have the power to close the door at any time,
removing the demons from my mind,
but they feed on me and control me.
So, I must remember to fight through the darkness,
because there's always light within it.
As soon as I remember I have the power to close the door,
the demons start to fade,
and the light returns and I'm in control again.
But I must find it in myself to always walk past the door,
ignoring all the familiar temptations.
For I know their strength and it's a battle every time,
but it's a battle that I have the power to win.
I just have to remember, it's only a door,
and doors can always be closed.

MAKE BELIEVE WORLD

Maybe I should get some help,
but how do I do that,
when I'm to blame,
for all this pain,
riddled inside my brain.
See I'm the problem,
in my tiny little world.
But that's the thing,
my world's a fantasy,
I conjured it up,
and made me the villain.
So, I never seek any help,
believing I'm to blame,
for all my struggles.
But really, it's just my brain,
once again playing games.
Because I'm not the villain,
or the problem.
I'm just being fed delusions,
from an unhealthy brain,
that's dealt with too much pain.
So, I need to stop placing the blame,
and give myself a break,
for it's just my brain playing a game.

SIMPLE WORDS

Funny how a few simple words can dismantle us completely,
even when we build ourselves up believing we are strong.
By telling ourselves not to sweat the small stuff,
and ignore the ones trying to bring us down.
Then before we know it our defenses are weakened,
from a few simple words that have slipped through the cracks.
Destroying who we are and making us feel under attack,
while taking away our confidence and ruining our pride.
For they want to get a rise out of us by making us feel small,
because then they feel better about themselves.
It's sad when damaged people go and hurt people,
by ridding us of our joy just because they're in pain.
For they know how to target our weak points,
and hit us where they know they'll destroy us.
But we need to stay strong and remember who we are,
and know that the words they say are twisted truths,
brought about to bring us pain.
For we are stronger than we could ever imagine,
from fighting our thoughts and fighting those around us.
Finding our inner strength will guide us,
as long as we stay true to ourselves.
Then we can fight the mind games,
by building up our defenses so they can't break us,
no matter how hard they try.
Because we are only as weak,
as we allow them to make us.

MOOD SWINGS

Some emotions are so strong,
you feel them,
deep within your bones.
They hit you like a wave,
overcome your senses,
and rattle you to your core,
while giving you mood swings,
you can no longer control.
Until you're irritational,
not making any sense,
even to yourself.
From being enraged,
and getting the shakes,
to falling so low,
you can't recognize your face,
or the words leaving your lips.
You're out of control,
and your mind is a circus.
But this isn't forever,
it's just temporary insanity.
For the anger will go away,
along with your sadness,
and the anxiety will subside.
Then you'll return to baseline,
where you're in control,
once again of your emotions.

HAPPY BEING ME

I just want to feel good enough,
and be proud of who I am,
but it's so hard when I can't get past,
every mistake that I've made.
They slowly eat at me,
tearing apart my self-esteem,
until there's none left.
So, I long for the feeling,
when I can finally be free,
of all these bad thoughts,
that I have about me.
When I can finally look in the mirror,
and I'm happy being me,
when I like all those little things,
that everyone likes about me.
It seems so easy to do,
but it's so hard for me,
to get past my own head,
and stop hating myself.
For I'm tired of this feeling,
where I'm not good enough,
to everyone and to me.
But I'll never be happy,
truly being me,
until I learn to appreciate,
all the unique things about me.
And learn to let go,
of all my mistakes,
only then will I feel good enough,
and happy being me.

MY DESTINATION

I set the GPS to my destination,
it looked like a simple ride.
But as I followed a straight path,
I found roadblocks along the way,
and a new detour every time.
An unsettling fog crept in,
and my GPS continued to reroute.
But it could barely keep up,
with all the new detours,
and there was never enough time,
to calculate a new route.
So, the GPS could no longer provide navigation,
and I got lost in an unknown direction,
while my destination got farther away.
There were too many unmarked roads ahead of me,
and each new road was bumpier than the last,
while the fog only got thicker.
Thus, I could barely see where I was going,
and anxiety built without a clear path,
until I was driving in circles,
not sure which way to go.
However, I remembered I had been lost before,
because the GPS always breaks,
and the fog always comes.
But my car is sturdy,
and it can handle the rocky roads.
In time the roads will get smoother,
and the fog will clear.
See the road always lead somewhere,
even if it's different from the original destination.
For the destination is never fully determined,
because there's always going to be roadblocks,
and new paths set up by detours.
Hence, the destination will always be unknown.

IT TAKES TIME

What's going on in my mind,
so much that you can't see,
all this internal conflict,
I hide from even me.
By telling myself I'm fine,
that I'll get through this,
just like the last time.
But my mental state is deteriorating,
and I think I finally cracked.
Maybe I should get some help,
but I give myself the disillusion,
all I need is a little more time,
for my happiness to return.
But what's taking so long,
I'm doing everything right,
but these things do take time.
Because I've been here before,
it doesn't happen overnight.
Though sometimes I've stumbled,
before I've gotten back up.
However, I will always survive,
if I never give up.

THE MOUNTAIN

The mountain seemed so small at first,
it was not a struggle to climb.
But as I climbed higher, it only got steeper,
my legs began to shake,
and my arms became weaker.
Until my hands could barely hang on,
and I slipped from the ridge.
Only saved by a last-minute grab of the rope,
that swung me out from the side of the mountain.
Then I came crashing back,
and bounced off the rocky ridges.
My body became battered and bruised,
and when the rope finally slipped from my hands,
I fell until it wrapped around my feet.
But as I hung there dangling,
with the ground out of sight,
and the top clearly in view.
I remembered the challenges I faced,
while climbing the mountain,
and all the time it had taken,
that I was not about to give up.
So, I found strength within myself,
and used the rope to pull me up.
Although I'm more wounded,
than I was when I began,
I'm now stronger than ever,
standing on top of the mountain,
amazed by the beauty of the view.

ACCEPTANCE

Some days I wake up feeling weak,
completely filled with defeat,
fighting with my mind,
which I have done a million times.
I have battled the world,
not just with myself,
been knocked to the ground,
and made to feel small.
Been taken advantage of,
and walked all over.
I've been abandoned,
and looked down upon.
Never seen as good enough,
and even to myself.
I have fixated on every flaw,
just a little too much,
and I have torn myself apart,
more times than I can count.
I have scars on my skin,
but more underneath,
and they tell the story of me,
that most never hear.
I'm always afraid of the stigma,
the judgment or the worry.
But the hardest acceptance,
is truly with myself.
Because I hate how I think,
always feeling like a burden.
My brain is full of dysfunction,
because my disorders built an army,
whose only mission is to destroy me.
But I can't change who I am,
or more so how I was built.
My traumas don't define me,
even though they helped shape me.
But I'm still here,
although I have had my doubts,
and I have gotten close to the edge.
I'll keep fighting this fight,
to find acceptance within myself.

THE MISSING PIECES

Broken and destroyed,
by the decisions you made.
Abandoned by your selfishness,
and left with an emptiness inside my heart.
All the fantasies of our future,
were destroyed in a second.
Dreams of you walking back into my life,
started to fade, and reality started to crack,
as every noise went silent.
The word dead echoed through my mind,
and instantly I joined a club I wanted no part of.
Taken by your own hand,
and overwhelmed with feelings of being left behind,
until the moment they showed up.
No longer was I alone,
for they seemed like superheroes,
coming to my rescue.
A family started to form,
while all the puzzle pieces came together.
No longer was I an only child,
for a world of possibilities opened.
You were gone forever,
but you left me six amazing gifts.
So, the darkness in my heart turned to light.
You may have broken me, but they saved me.

WINDOW OF MY PAST

As I peer into the window of my past,
I can see myself,
sitting in a chair, cold, frightened, and alone.
Fear is visible on my face,
but I can feel the wanting to belong.
Just left feeling completely invisible and ignored,
while feeling weak, just crawling in my skin.
Constantly looking over my shoulder,
like I was being watched,
with whispers behind my back as I was mocked.
I wanted to get away,
because I didn't know who I was,
or who I was turning into.
The cells in my body were all out of sorts,
and I wanted so badly to run away.
Because I felt like I was only in the way,
and there was no need for me at all.
So, I felt empty,
nothing about me felt right,
and all I saw were giants around me,
because I felt so small.
However, that is no longer me, or my life,
so, I must back away from this window.
For it's a representation of my past,
not of my current life,
because I have found myself,
and where I belong.
Now everything feels so different,
because I finally feel free.
It may have taken some time to get here,
but I'm finally content,
and I'm comfortable being me.

CLEAN SLATE

What if we could forget who we are,
even if just for a moment,
and have all our memories stripped away,
while being left as a blank slate.
No longer remembering the trauma,
and all the pain brought on by others.
Not to mention the hurt we've inflicted,
and all the residual guilt left behind,
while forgetting the ones we've lost.
Imagine getting knocked out,
and given temporary amnesia.
We wouldn't relive all our mistakes,
or think about our regrets.
No more replaying conversations,
or stupid decisions we've made.
The pain would no longer be there,
because it would be forgotten.
We would no longer wish to be someone else,
because the old us would be gone.
Replaced with someone new and innocent,
completely free of our trauma and mistakes.
It would be nice if we could forget,
imagine all the relief we'd feel,
even if it was just for a day.

INNOCENCE

Seems like only yesterday,
when we were different.
Before the walls got built around us,
meant to protect us,
have now closed off our hearts.
Keeping us always guarded,
for fear of letting in a Trojan Horse.
So, now we push everyone away,
and the lonelier we feel.
Never truly connecting,
or embracing the comfort we deserve.
The innocence when we were young,
it seems so far gone now.
All that good we saw in people,
before it got beaten out of us,
has all but faded away.
We're no longer filled with trust,
now everyone has a motive.
Everyone seeks to use and abuse us,
and we're so afraid to be hurt,
that nobody is allowed in.
Thus, we're only growing colder,
slowly becoming more disconnected.
If only there was a way to recapture the magic,
the hearts we had when we were young.
Imagine the kind of people we would become,
and the society we would have.

HAPPINESS IN A BOTTLE

If only we could capture happiness in a bottle,
and use it whenever we feel down.
Because when hope starts dwindling,
and those demons come back around,
wouldn't it be nice to recapture that spark.
A glimmer of happiness when it's hard to find.
But imagine drinking from that bottle,
or sipping on it like a fine wine,
that would instantly bring us to a time,
when everything was good,
and the bad was hard to find.
Then the mind would reset,
and give us relief,
while pushing the demons away.
Oh, if we could capture happiness in a bottle,
imagine how easier life would be.
But at least we have our memories,
which can help ease our mind,
by warming our hearts, and reminding us,
happiness is never out of reach.

RETURNING TO THE LIGHT

MENTAL ILLNESS STIGMA

I wish mental illness could be seen,
because it's a sickness, it's a disease,
it's just one you can't see.
If only you could see the bandages,
wrapped around the sick,
and it wasn't so looked down upon,
more people would feel less alone.
Because nobody can see the pain,
without the crutches and casts,
it's seen so differently.
There are never any cards,
or sympathy for the pain,
because to the masses,
it's just not understood.
So many don't reach out,
for fear of being judged.
If only there was no stigma,
and people could be fully open,
then they wouldn't feel so empty.
Because it's a cruel world out there,
and they shouldn't have to do it alone.
We need to band together,
remove the judgment, and just listen.
Because the wounded need empathy,
not more scars.

NOT ALONE

Sometimes the weight is too much to bear,
always feeling crushed and living in despair.
Feeling misunderstood and completely alone,
afraid to reach out because of the unknown.
Not knowing how you'll be perceived,
from being told it could always be worse,
or being micromanaged on how to process,
all the traumas you've been through,
that most will never know.
Because nobody has walked in your shoes,
but you are not alone.
There're so many people out there,
wearing a mask on their face.
Hiding all their pain for fear of rejection,
and terrified the view of them will change,
if they finally take off their mask.
Thinking they'll be seen as damaged goods,
because the stigma is real and it's all around.
There is never a set healing time,
so people just don't understand,
why it's taking you so long to get better,
and they'll think you aren't trying.
But nobody understands your internal battles,
except for the people living behind their masks,
a hidden society of pain scared to connect.
No two battles are the same,
and everyone processes things differently.
But I have lived just like you,
and there have been so many days,
I've forgotten how to breathe.
Just living in fear of everything and everyone,
and always feeling like a problem,
never knowing who I can trust,
with my lifetime of darkness.
Time may not heal all wounds,
but there will be better days,
even if they seem far away.
Remember you are never alone,
even if it feels that way and I should know,
because I'm someone like you.

ONE MORE DAY

You've been struggling for so long,
that the battle feels all but lost,
and countless times,
you've wanted to give up.
However, you're still here,
even though each day,
has been harder than the last.
You've made it through,
to feel the wind on your face,
and the heat from the sun.
Remember the little wins,
because they'll keep you strong.
So, don't give up,
when there could be a reason,
just waiting for you tomorrow,
to make you glad you stayed,
even for just one more day.
For the unknown is terrifying,
but it's also the reason that you should stay.
Because what's around the corner,
could be the one thing that takes away the pain.
So, you must hold on for one more day.
Even though it's unknown, when the day will come,
that makes you happy, for sticking it out,
through all those bad days.
But it will come, and make you say,
I'm glad I stayed, just to see another day.

WARRIOR

Living under a shadow of darkness,
behind a perfect smile lives a shattered girl.
A seemingly perfect life above the surface,
but underneath she fights monsters and demons,
on a battlefield that nobody can see.
Even when her chances of winning are slim,
she keeps on fighting,
while the demons manifest in her mind.
Because she is a warrior,
and the sound of her battle cry keeps her strong,
while pushing away the monsters in her brain.
Even though nobody can see her pain,
or the wounds she carries, she is not a quitter.
No matter how much darkness surrounds her,
nor how broken she becomes,
because she is a survivor,
and she fights to the very end.
For it's her life at stake,
and no matter how difficult the battles become,
she knows it's a life worth fighting for.

MY PRESENCE

Some days I feel like I'm barely holding on,
getting in my head that I'm nothing but weak,
but then I remember I'm still here.
There's so much strength in my presence,
and even though I brush it off,
the heartbeat in my chest is a reminder.
I'm so much stronger than I think,
constantly surprising even myself,
but never giving myself the credit I deserve.
There've been so many hidden battles,
and not all have been flawless victories,
but the battle that's always there,
can only be won by still being here.
The battle of just existing,
especially in the face of adversity,
because it's easy to get lost sometimes,
and I may never be perfect,
or filled with a cheery disposition.
There are times I may be falling apart,
and bursting with complete negativity.
But at the end of the day, I'm still fighting,
even when the odds are stacked against me,
from people trying to bring me down,
or from my broken mind creating a false reality.
My presence will always be a reminder,
if I'm still here, then I'm winning.

BREAKING THROUGH

You just want to be free,
and get rid of the worries and the pain,
while removing all the strain that's tearing your life apart.
Which is hard when all your instincts say to hide,
and your inner voice says go against the grain,
bury your fears and fight to see the brighter days.
But just when you're at your lowest, life can be surprising,
it's like the world is trying to show you something,
but you have been too blind to see it.
So, when you're ready to give up and forget about life,
it gives you a reason to keep fighting.
But you must be willing to go through some pain,
a metaphysical journey of self-reflection.
It's an endless internal battle of questioning,
and the demon on your shoulder will say you're weak,
try and play games and trick you to admit defeat,
but the insanity you feel will subside.
There's no instruction manual to guide you,
but find your purpose, a reason to stay strong.
For staying true to yourself in the face of opposition,
will allow you to truly break through to the other side.

HAPPINESS AND SADNESS

It's hard for happiness to exist without sadness,
when you need sadness to appreciate happiness.
So don't get upset with yourself,
when you feel a little down.
Because when happiness comes back around,
you'll feel it in a new way,
from spending some time away.
For they need to coexist, to give life to the other.
Because you'd never know true happiness,
if you didn't experience a little trauma,
and how would you understand sadness,
if you never experienced joy.
For the emotions balance each other out,
and always stay close by,
even when it's the other's turn.
So, while sadness may seem in control,
remember happiness is just around the corner,
to give sadness a little break.
It's never totally in control,
because happiness is always in the background,
and sadness is just having its turn.
But wait until you feel happy,
it'll be more amazing,
when it finally gets its turn.

LETTING OTHERS IN

Underneath the surface is where they hide,
all the feelings you conceal from the world.
The you that nobody really knows,
with all the broken pieces you bury deep inside,
terrified to bring to the surface.
So, you hide them away in the light of day.
You bury your feelings when you're visible,
because we tend to hide who we really are.
Only ever letting in a select few,
but even then, they never get the whole story.
Now imagine a world,
where we could be our true selves.
Never needing to suppress our feelings,
or hiding the deepest parts of ourselves.
For there would be no judgment,
it would be an open world of understanding,
and we wouldn't be afraid to connect with others.
But to connect, we need to peel back our layers,
and find others just like us, the ones we can trust.
Only then can we open ourselves up,
while we tear down some of our walls.
Because it gets lonely hiding from the world,
and the real you that lives underneath the surface,
is more beautiful than you realize.
No matter how broken you see yourself,
you are special just the way you are.

ROLLERCOASTER

Speeding, faster, and faster,
on the roller coaster of life,
with each passing turn,
memories of the past,
flash before your eyes.
Those days are long gone,
but so much has happened,
and the pain must not be forgotten.
For the tears were never a waste,
because they made you who you are.
Hold onto the memories with your friends,
even friends that are no longer on the ride,
and laugh at the stupid things you did with them.
Cherish all the good memories,
but don't linger in the past.
You'll miss what's all around you,
and it may feel like you hit a wall,
because facing what's in front of you is hard.
Even though the ride is scary,
you must keep your eyes open,
because you can't sleep through this.
You must wake up before it's too late,
it's the only life you have.
For there will always be sharp turns,
trying to throw you off the tracks.
But the ride will never slow down,
and you will never be able to get off.
For time will never stop,
and there will always be hills to climb.
But you must believe in yourself,
because there is always a new turn,
and within each turn is a new beginning.
Adapt to the change in momentum,
and try to use the past to guide you.
But never let it take control of you,
because reality is in the present,
it's waiting for you on the tracks.
So, keep your eyes open,
and never forget to hold on.
Just remember to always breathe,
for each track is temporary,
and there will always be another turn.

CHOICES

Life moves so fast sometimes,
that we can get lost in it.
Appreciate the seconds,
and the minutes that pass,
no matter how small.
Each moment is precious,
and the people that enter our lives,
all serve a purpose.
Everyone is important,
and the encounters we have,
can be good or bad.
However, they factor into our identity,
and help define who we are.
The kindness or brutality they display,
can make us weak or strong.
But it's all how we face each situation,
because there's no right way to live.
But we're given choices,
and we can choose to be a good person,
amidst the struggles we encounter.
The right road to travel is not always clear,
but kindness and forgiveness should always prevail,
over hate and resentment.
There're always multiple roads,
so, choose your path carefully.

THE MAZE

Life is a mystery set up to be explored,
with never-ending spirals,
built deep within the design.
It's a maze filled with danger,
but within it are so many beautiful secrets,
that can only be unraveled with a clear mind.
So, use your mind as your compass,
and get in touch with your soul.
There's a secret strength within all of us,
and to be authentic, you must take off your mask.
It's the only way to connect with the world around you,
so, stop playing games with yourself.
You may stumble along the way,
trying to find the person hidden deep inside,
but you are stronger than you realize.
So, wipe away the pain and dust off your face,
because you are hiding how beautiful you are.
And to truly live, you need to open your eyes,
by running towards what's scary.
There's always a chance of pain,
but let yourself feel passion, and embrace love,
take deep breaths, and fight through the maze.
Don't look back and don't give up,
just try to find the light within yourself,
by clearing a path in your mind.
Have faith in yourself to get up,
no matter how many times you fall,
because the maze will never end.
But if you keep walking,
you'll always be closer to enlightenment.
Serenity is just on the other side,
of all the darkest parts of your mind.
So, keep walking,
and you'll be stronger, and wiser,
for the rest of your journey through the maze.

PERCEPTION

For the future I could not see,
and the past I let define me,
my present was waiting to begin.
If only I stopped to look,
and if I started to listen,
I would no longer be lost in past mistakes,
but I would live without hesitation.
Then for a moment time would stop,
and the beauty of all the wondrous,
and small forgotten nothingness,
would then ignite a fury of importance,
that would have remained invisible and unknown.
For your biggest challenges and impossible struggles,
will give you a life worth living.
Then you will make sense of the dark,
and the light will be fully appreciated,
while you will reach a level of wisdom,
that would never have been achieved.

MASTERPIECE

We're all works of art,
special masterpieces in progress.
Like an unfinished painting,
nobody knows how we'll look,
until the final brushstroke.
Along the way there'll be mistakes,
errors to be corrected.
However, it's impossible to see the final product,
while we're still being painted.
So, it's best not to judge an unfinished painting,
because even a few imperfections,
can make a painting better in the end.
For they're all unique in some way,
from the brushstrokes to the color palate.
They all have their differences,
and beauty to admire.
The process to the final product can be long.
But no matter what the final product is,
all the corrections and new ideas,
scribbled on the page,
will create a beautiful work of art.
A masterpiece to be proud of.

STRENGTH WITHIN THE STRUGGLE

There's beauty to the darkness that only some can see.
A certain appreciation to the light,
gifted to those that have been lost in the dark.
The ones lost in the dark developed a flashlight to see,
a means to make their way back into the light.
The struggles they faced not only made them stronger,
but it also opened their eyes.
All the beauty that surrounds us every day,
is hidden while lost in the dark,
with all focus being placed on survival.
However, when the struggle has died down,
and they finally stand back in the light,
it's like the world is brighter, and more colorful.
The world feels transformed into something else,
and there's magic to everything that was once hidden.
But the only way to see this beauty requires a little pain,
from internal and external battles of devastation.
Because without it, the beauty gets missed,
by the ones that haven't been lost in the dark.
For their eyes were never fully opened,
to truly appreciate everything around them.
Coming out of the darkness is like coming up for air,
everything feels, smells, and tastes better,
because for so long all those things were lost.
They should never be ashamed of their dark past,
because it has made them who they are,
and it has gifted them with an appreciation for life,
that they never had before.
Now they are truly living,
and they have a strength inside themselves,
that could only be found within their struggles.

AUTHOR BIO

Margaux B. Scott grew up in Rhode Island and always aspired to do something creative. She always excelled in the arts whether it be drawing or writing. As a child she made up newspaper stories, by writing articles as well as drawing illustrations. She took her aspirations in art and received a Bachelor's Degree in Graphic Design from Rhode Island College. While trying to capitalize in the field, she received an Associate's Degree in Web Development and Programming from the Community College of Rhode Island. Although she never majored in writing, she took every opportunity to expand her craft by taking elective Creative Writing classes in high school and college.

Writing has always stayed a consistent hobby due to it being used as an outlet for any struggles she has faced in her life. Throughout her life, she has suffered from anxiety, ADHD, and depression, with writing being one of the few things that has given her inner peace. Besides writing, she has also found comfort in video games, art, and aggressive inline skating. She has always tried to experiment with different genres of writing, from creating short stories and works of fiction to poetry. One of her main inspirations in creating this book was the chance to help people, which she has always aspired to do. Sometimes the simplest way to help others is to make them feel less alone and that others relate to them. Knowing she is not the only one that thinks like she does, she figured opening herself up would allow others to do the same and reach out if they needed help, and she could merge her two passions, writing and helping others.

www.ingramcontent.com/pod-product-compliance
Lightning Source LLC
Chambersburg PA
CBHW071237090426
42736CB00014B/3120